Grey Cup

Kaite Goldsworthy

Weigl

Published by Weigl Educational Publishers Limited
6325 10th Street SE
Calgary, Alberta T2H 2Z9
Website: www.weigl.com

Library and Archives Canada Cataloguing in Publication

Goldsworthy, Kaite
          Grey Cup / written by Kaite Goldsworthy.
(Canadian icons)
Includes index.
ISBN 978-1-77071-664-3 (bound).--ISBN 978-1-77071-670-4 (pbk.)
               1. Grey Cup (Football)--Juvenile literature.
I. Title. II. Series: Canadian icons

GV948.G65 2011   j796.335'648   C2011-900809-2

Printed in the United States of America in North Mankato, Minnesota
1 2 3 4 5 6 7 8 9 0 15 14 13 12 11

052011
WEP37500

Editor: Heather Kissock
Art Director: Terry Paulhus

Weigl acknowledges Alamy, the Canadian Football Hall of Fame and Museum, Corbis, and Getty Images as image suppliers for this title.

Every reasonable effort has been made to trace ownership and to obtain permission to reprint copyright material. The publishers would be pleased to have any errors or omissions brought to their attention so that they may be corrected in subsequent printings.

We acknowledge the financial support of the Government of Canada through the Canada Book Fund for our publishing activities.

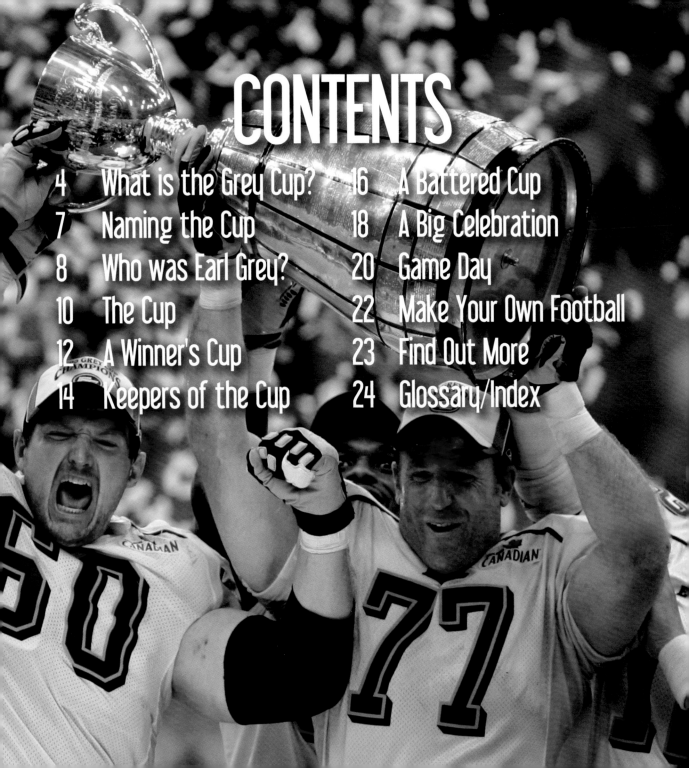

CONTENTS

What is the Grey Cup?

The Grey Cup is the most important trophy in the **Canadian Football League (CFL)**. Every year, the top team from eastern Canada plays the top team from the west. The winner of the game wins the Grey Cup.

5

6

Naming the Cup

The Grey Cup is named after Earl Grey. He was Canada's ninth **governor general**. In 1909, Earl Grey donated the cup as an award for the top **rugby** football team in Canada. The first Grey Cup game was held December 4, 1909, in Toronto, Ontario.

Who was Earl Grey?

Earl Grey was the governor general of Canada from 1904 to 1911. Earl Grey worked hard to **unite** Canada and its people. He set up several awards to honour sports and the arts in Canada. In 1963, he was **elected** into the Canadian Football Hall of Fame for his contribution to football.

9

The Cup

The Grey Cup was made in 1909. At first, it was just a silver cup on a wooden base. Over time, pieces have been added to it. The cup is now much larger.

When the cup was made, it cost about $48.00. It is now worth about $75,000.00.

A Winner's Cup

Each year, the names of the winning team and its members are **engraved** on metal plaques. These plaques are attached to the base of the cup.

The winning team keeps the cup for two months. It is then sent to the Canadian Football Hall of Fame in Hamilton, Ontario. There, it is put on display for people to see. It often tours the country as well.

Keepers of the Cup

Two people take care of the Grey Cup whenever it travels. These people must keep the cup near them at all times. Besides members of the winning team, they are the only people allowed to pick up the trophy. Fans may have their photos taken with the trophy, but the handlers remain close by.

A Battered Cup

The Grey Cup has not always been treated well. The trophy has been broken several times. It survived a fire in 1947. In 1969, it was stolen and held for **ransom**.

Since then, a **replica** of the Grey Cup has been made. It is displayed at the Canadian Football Hall of Fame when the real cup is on tour.

A Big Celebration

The Grey Cup game is held every November. It is held in a different city each year. The Grey Cup game is a time to celebrate. The host city often plans concerts and parties. These events take place the week before the game is played.

Game Day

The Grey Cup game is watched by millions of people. Some go to the game. Others watch it on television. When the game is over, the Grey Cup is given to the winning team.

A few days after the game, the winning city holds a parade for its team. The Grey Cup is a special guest at the parade.

Make Your Own Football

Supplies

brown paper bag

tape

white glue

scissors

pencil

white paper

1. Lay the paper bag flat. Draw a large football shape on one side of the bag. Cut the shape from both sides of the bag. When complete, you should have two football-shaped pieces of paper. Put the leftover scraps of paper aside for now.

2. Carefully tape the edges of your football together, leaving an opening on one side.

3. Stuff the leftover paper scraps into your football. Be careful not to overstuff your football or it might tear. When you have finished stuffing, tape the football closed.

4. To make the football's stitches, cut one thick strip and six short rectangles out of the white paper. Glue the thick strip lengthwise in the middle of the football. Then, glue the single strips across the thick strip. Now you are ready for a touchdown!

Find Out More

To learn more about the Grey Cup, visit these websites.

The Canadian Football League
www.cflgreycup.ca

Grey Cup—The Fans and the Fanfare
http://archives.cbc.ca/sports/football/
topics/381/

**Archives of the Governor
General of Canada**
archive.gg.ca/gg/fgg/bios/01/
grey_e.asp

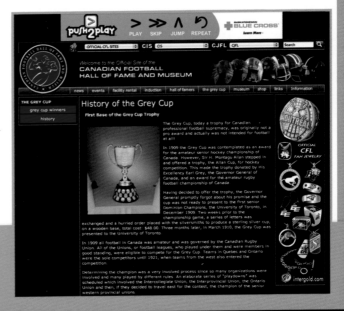

Canadian Football Hall of Fame
www.cfhof.ca/page/
history_grey_cup

Glossary

Canadian Football League (CFL): an organization for professional Canadian football teams

elected: chosen by a vote

engraved: marked or written on a hard surface

governor general: a person who represents the queen in Canada

ransom: a demand for money to return something of value

replica: an exact copy

rugby: a type of football game

unite: to bring together

Index